Faces YOU SEE in the Forest

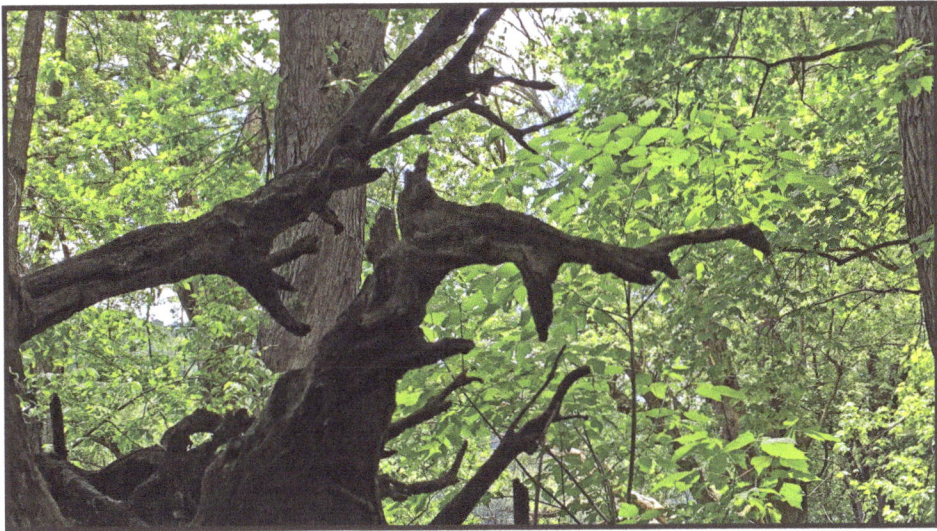

Photos and Text by
Amy Stewart-Wilmarth

Surrogate Press®

Faces YOU SEE in the Forest began many years ago when my sons and I were hiking in the woods and we came across a tree with sturdy low branches, a tree perfect for climbing! Nearby was a thick, old tree with an odd shaped rock lying next to it. Because of the rock's position to this tree it looked like a tongue sticking out!

What do you see?

_____

_____

_____

Through the years many more "faces" and "creatures" have been discovered in unusual wooded habitats.

I would like to share my favorite ones with you as creative writing prompts or purely for your imagination. I have included my own interpretations of these woodland faces. What are yours? No interpretation is wrong and few are the same.

What do you see?

_____

_____

_____

_____

_____

❀ ❀ ❀ ❀ ❀

I see an elephant trumpeting
an early morning revelry
out to the Forest's creatures.

What do you see?

_____

_____

_____

_____

_____

✾ ✾ ✾ ✾ ✾

I see an angry face!
This angry face tree watches over the Forest.
Could it be a wizard?

What do you see?

_____

_____

_____

_____

_____

❧ ❧ ❧ ❧ ❧

I see a small monster who took
a wrong turn out of the Forest.
I think she enjoys the quiet shoreline.

What do you see?

_____

_____

_____

_____

_____

🍃 🍃 🍃 🍃 🍃

I see a raptor who has stopped to take
a quick look around before she darts off!
Where is she going now?

What do you see?

_____

_____

_____

_____

_____

❧ ❧ ❧ ❧ ❧

I see a happy go lucky whistler of beautiful
songs that float throughout the Forest.
Maybe he can cheer up the angry face tree?

What do you see?

_____

_____

_____

_____

_____

🍃 🍃 🍃 🍃 🍃

I see two alligators relaxing by the Forest's
cool river with the warm sun
soaking into their scaly backs.

What do you see?

_____

_____

_____

_____

_____

🍃 🍃 🍃 🍃 🍃

I see a screamer!
I bet he woke up the entire forest!

What do you see?

_____

_____

_____

_____

_____

❧ ❧ ❧ ❧ ❧

I see a shimmering big fin fish
diving back into the water.

What do you see?

_____

_____

_____

_____

_____

❧ ❧ ❧ ❧ ❧

I see a turkey hiding behind a thinning bush.
She remains perfectly still.
Do you think she heard me?

What do you see?

_____

_____

_____

_____

_____

❧ ❧ ❧ ❧ ❧

I see a frog that hops all over the Forest!
He leaves his tongue hanging out
ready for plump, juicy flies and bugs
to come by and get stuck!

What do you see?

_____

_____

_____

_____

_____

🍃 🍃 🍃 🍃 🍃

I see a buffalo skeleton.
He looks very comfortable relaxing
in the cool dirt. Did you know that buffalos
love rolling around in dirt?

What do you see?

_____

_____

_____

_____

_____

🍂 🍂 🍂 🍂 🍂

I see an antelope resting
on a soft bed of colorful leaves.

What do you see?

_____

_____

_____

_____

_____

🌿 🌿 🌿 🌿 🌿

I see a coiling snake. Is he ready to strike?
Or is he stretching in the warm sunshine.
Either way, I will keep my distance.

What do you see?

_____

_____

_____

_____

_____

🍃 🍃 🍃 🍃 🍃

I see a rhinoceros wading along the river's
edge chomping on delicious grasses.
Did you know that a rhinoceros has toe nails?

What do you see?

_____

_____

_____

_____

_____

✿ ✿ ✿ ✿ ✿

Oh no, I see another rhinoceros!
Will they be friends or foes?
I think they will be great pals.

What do you see?

_____

_____

_____

_____

_____

_____

🍃 🍃 🍃 🍃 🍃

I see an enormous gray mouse looking out
over a busy park. Did you know a mouse can
squeeze through a hole about the size
of a dime? I doubt this one can!

What do you see?

_____

_____

_____

_____

_____

✦ ✦ ✦ ✦ ✦

I see a young girl with curls that frame her face.
Her lighthearted smile and wide-open eyes lead
me to believe she has discovered something
special in the forest. I wonder what she sees?
Could there be more faces in the Forest?

About the Author and Photographer

Amy Stewart-Wilmarth enjoys writing and photography as paths for expressing sentiments, life events and capturing nature's beauty. She exhibits at the annual Leonard J. Buck Garden Art Exhibit in NJ and her photography was published online in 2007 and 2012. She wrote and photographed her first book, Along the Morris Canal in 2014 and was a contributor and photographer for the book Growing Up Laker; A Collective Memoir of the First 70 Years published in 2019.

Amy has a degree in Nursing and a B.A in Psychology. She is a certified Holistic Health Coach and has focused her nursing career on nutrition, prevention and senior advocacy. She presently works for an organization as their Health and Wellness Director. She lives in New Jersey and enjoys the outdoors including being a longtime supporter of organizations dedicated to protecting marine life on the East Coast.

Acknowledgements

This enduring and sentimental collection of woodland faces is dedicated to my sons and our many years of fun exploring. And I am grateful to Rick Wilmarth, and Alex and Jamie Reilly for their keen editing skills and support.

❧ ❧ ❧ ❧ ❧

Published in the United States by Surrogate Press® an imprint of Faceted Press®
Surrogate Press, LLC, Park City, Utah
www.SurrogatePresss.com

Library of Congress Control Number: 2020914016
ISBN: 978-1-947459-43-4

Printed in the United States of America

Book design by Surrogate Press®

www.ingramcontent.com/pod-product-compliance
Lightning Source LLC
Chambersburg PA
CBHW051312020426

42333CB00027B/3306